W9-CYW-061

100

5

© 1989 Modern Publishing, a division of Unisystems, Inc.

™ A Preschool Read•A•Picture Book is a trademark owned by
Modern Publishing, a division of Unisystems, Inc.

® Honey Bear Books is a trademark owned by Honey Bear Productions, Inc.,
and is registered in the U.S. Patent and Trademark Office.

No part of this book may be reproduced or copied without written
approval from the publisher. All Rights Reserved

Printed in U.S.A.

A Preschool Read·A·Picture Book™

Little Kids in the Neighborhood

Written by Jeffie Ross Gordon
Illustrated by Mary Ann Fraser

MODERN PUBLISHING
A Division of Unisystems, Inc.
New York, NY 10022

Table of Contents

MOTHER GOOSE

WILD ANIMALS

TRUCKS

FAIRY TALES

BEARS

DINOSAURS

LONG AGO

DOGS

Good Books

Words for Good Books

 Emmy

 dinosaurs

 Ethan

 bears

 library

 trucks

 book

Good Books

Lisa, the baby sitter, took  and and Scott to the .

"Please help me find a to read," said .

"Here is a with pictures of ," said Lisa.

"I do not want that ," said .

"Here is a with pictures of ," said .

"I do not want that ," said .

"Here is a with pictures of ," said Scott.

"I do not want that ," said .

"Here is a with words," said Lisa.

"Thank you," said . "That is the I want."

11

Mother's Office

New words for Mother's Office

 Mother

 telephone

 chair

 Father

 desk

Words you have learned

 Ethan

 Emmy

Mother's Office

"Today, we are going to my office," said.

In the office, there was a , a and a .

"I want to sit in the ," said .

"The spins around and around," said .

 climbed onto the .

 spun the around.

"That was fun," said .

"Now it is my turn," said .

 climbed onto the and spun the around.

Then the rang, and sat in her . answered the .

"It is on the ," said . " is going to meet us for lunch."

and were very happy.

Open Wide

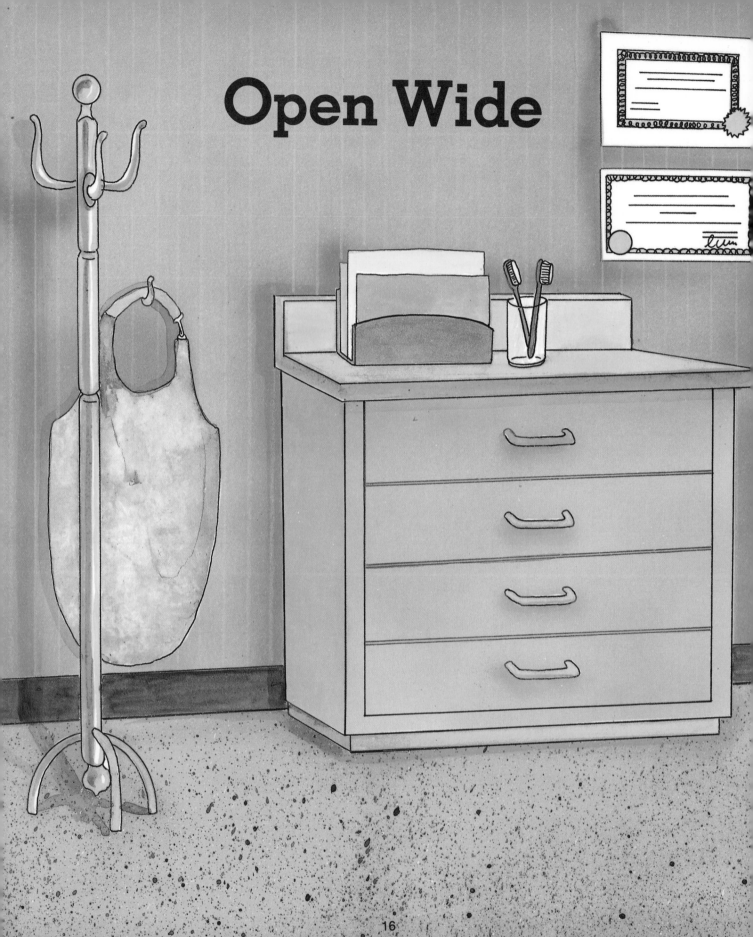

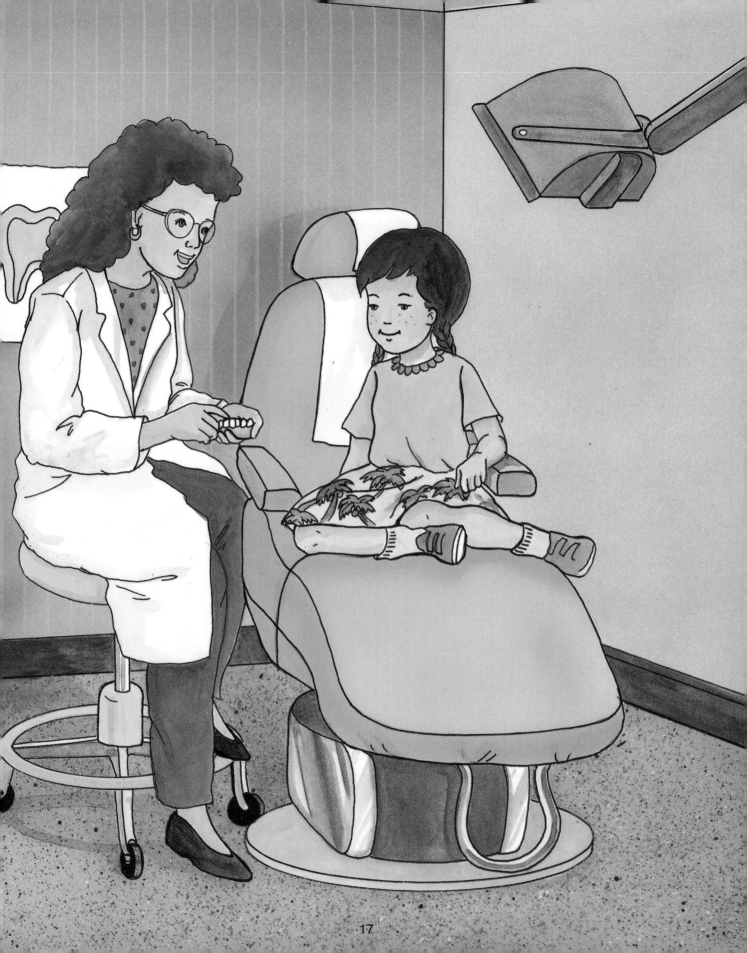

New words for Open Wide

 teeth

 cookies

 toothbrush

 Pooch

Words you have learned

 Emmy

 Father

 Ethan

 Mother

Open Wide

 and went to their dentist, Doctor Kate.

"Open wide, ," said Doctor Kate. Doctor Kate looked at her .

"Your turn, ," said Doctor Kate. Doctor Kate looked at his .

 and , do you use your every day?" asked Doctor Kate.

"Every day," said .

" says we have to brush our every day," said .

"And you should not eat too many ," said Doctor Kate.

" does not let us eat too many ," said .

"You are taking good care of your . You have no cavities," said

Doctor Kate.

"I bet  has cavities," said . "He does not have a ."

"And he loves ," said .

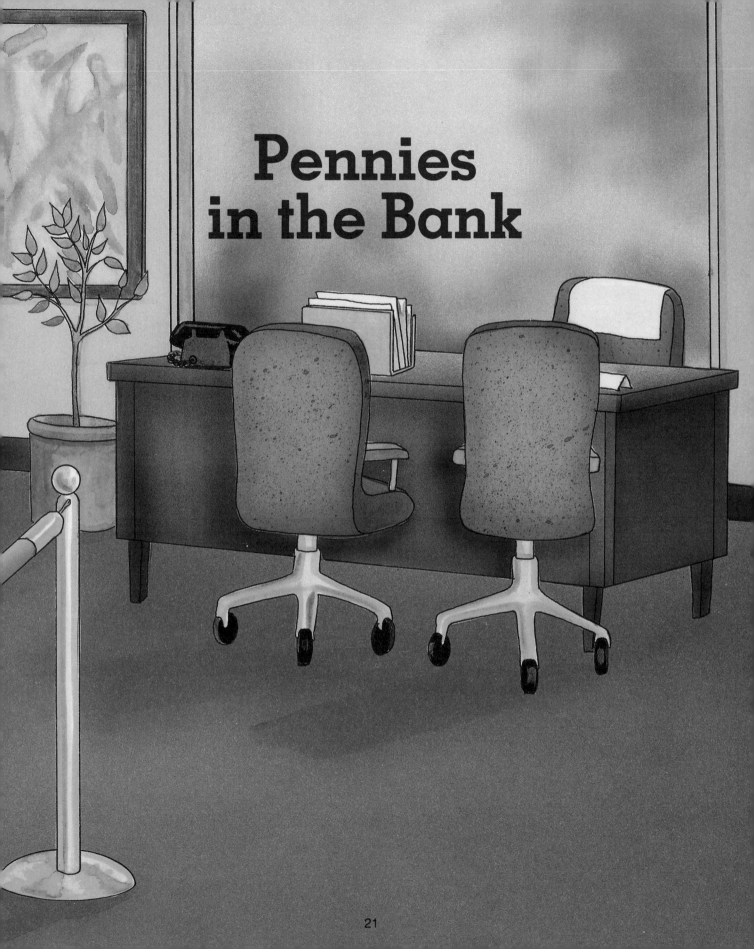

Pennies
in the Bank

New words for Pennies in the Bank

 piggy bank

 pig

 car

Words you have learned

 Ethan

 chair

 Father

 Mother

 desk

Pennies in the Bank

"Your is full of pennies, ," said . "We will take the pennies to the big bank."

 and rode in the 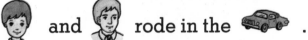 .

They stopped at a big building. It was the bank.

Inside, saw a . He saw a like had in her office. He saw people waiting in a long line. He did not see any pennies.

"This does not look like a bank," said .

"What does a bank look like?" asked .

"A bank looks like a ," said .

"This is not a . This is a big bank," said .

"I cannot leave my pennies at this bank," said .

"Why?" asked .

"Because there is no hole to put the pennies in," said .

laughed.

23

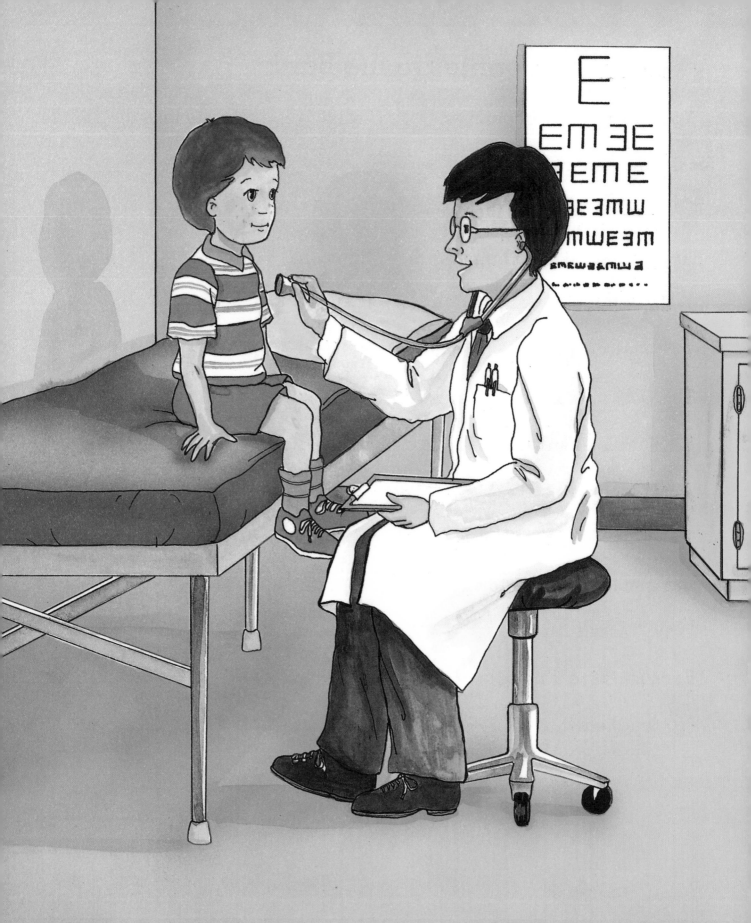

Doctor
Tom

New words for Doctor Tom

 table

600 six hundred

100 one hundred

 ears

5 five

eyes

 fingers

200 two hundred

Words you have learned

Emmy

 Father

 book

 Mother

 Ethan

Doctor Tom

At Doctor Tom's office, read a  to .

"I do not want to visit Doctor Tom," said .

"But today is your checkup, " said . "I like Doctor Tom. And you will like him, too. Doctor Tom is our friend."

"Doctor Tom is ready, ," said Nurse Ann. sat on a long .

"You are getting very tall," said Doctor Tom. "How old are you now, ?
You must be **100** ."

 laughed. "I am **5** ," said . He held up **5** .

" **5** already. Soon you will be older than I am," said Doctor Tom.

"No," said . "You must be **600** ."

"How did you know?" asked Doctor Tom.

"You are bigger than me. You are big like ," said .

Doctor Tom told to sit still. Doctor Tom looked at his 👂 . Then he looked at his 👁 👁 . "You are very healthy, ," said Doctor Tom.

 left Doctor Tom's office. and were in the waiting room.

"You were right, ," said . "I like Doctor Tom. I will come back when I am **200** ."

The Police Station

516
POLICE

New words for The Police Station

 shirt

 pants

 hat

 badge

 police car

 street

 motorcycle

 horses

 milk

Words you have learned

 Ethan

 cookies

30

The Police Station

Scott's dad was a policeman. He wore a blue , blue and a blue

police . He had a silver . One day, he took Scott and to

visit the police station.

Scott and rode in the .

Scott's dad turned on the red light on top of the . The siren made a

loud noise.

Scott and waved to the people on the .

At the police station, one policeman had a and some policemen

had . All of the policemen talked to and Scott.

Scott's dad gave Scott and   and .

"Policemen are nice. I would like to be a policeman when I grow up," said

.

"Me, too," said Scott. "I want to be just like my dad."

Shopping at the Market

New words for Shopping at the Market

 shopping cart

 bananas

 bread

 cherries

 eggs

 1 one

 bone

 apple

Words you have learned

 Mother

 milk

 Father

Pooch

Ethan

 cookies

 Emmy

Shopping at the Market

and and and went shopping at the market.

walked up the aisles and down the aisles.

pushed the .

and helped push the .

put and in the . She put in and a for

.

put in the . He put in and .

"May I put something in the ?" asked .

"You may put **1** thing in the ," said .

put an in the .

"May I put something in the ?" asked .

"You also may put **1** thing in the ," said .

"I want to put me in the ," said . "Shopping has made me too

tired to walk."

The Post Office

New words for The Post Office

 box

 airplane

 stamps

 house

 mail bag

 letter

 mail truck

Words you have learned

 Emmy

 Ethan

The Post Office

 and took a trip to the post office.

"May I help you?" asked the lady at the counter.

"We would like to mail a to our grandma," said .

"How will this get to our grandma?" asked .

"I will put on the ," said the lady. "I will put the in a . A will take the to the airport. Then the will go on the ."

"But how does it get to grandma's ?" asked .

"Well, another will take the to the post office in your grandma's town," said the lady. "The post office will take the out of the . A mailperson will deliver this to your grandma."

"That sounds like fun," said 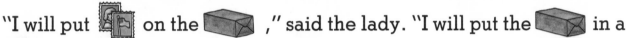 . "Please put  on me and mail me to Grandma."

"We cannot mail little boys," said the lady . "But we can mail a . You can write a to your grandma."

"He does not know how to write," said . "But I will help him."

"That's a good idea," said the post office lady.

New words for Fire Station Field Trip

 fire station

 fire hose

 coats

 fire hydrant

 fire hats

 fire ladders

 boots

 fire dog

 fire truck

Words you have learned

 Emmy

Fire Station Field Trip

 and Jane went to the with their class.

"The fire bell rings when there is a fire," said Firefighter Mary. "We move very fast."

"We slide down the pole," said Firefighter Steven.

"We put on long , and tall ," said Firefighter Jack.

"Then what happens?" asked .

"We climb into the . At the fire, we hook the to the ," said Firefighter Steven. "Then we put the up against the building. We can put out the fire."

"What does the do?" asked .

"The keeps us company at the ," said Firefighter Sylvia.

"Well, I like the the best," said Jane.

"I like the the best," said .

Words You Have Learned in Little Kids in the Neighborhood

Emmy
Ethan
library
dinosaurs
bears
trucks
book
Mother

chair
desk
telephone
Father
teeth
toothbrush
cookies
Pooch
piggy bank
pig
car
one hundred
five
fingers
six hundred
ears
eyes
two hundred
table
shirt
pants

hat
badge
police car
street
motorcycle
horses
milk
shopping cart
bread
eggs
bone
bananas
cherries
one
apple
box
stamps
mail bag
mail truck
airplane
letter

house
fire station
coats
fire hats
boots
fire truck
fire hose
fire hydrant
fire ladders
fire dog